South Yorkshire of Pontefract 1925 to 1994

Part One: 1929 to 1973: Birth and Consolidation

Stuart Emmett

I hope you enjoy the journey through this book which has been very pleasurable to research and write and could not have happened without the many wonderful photographers who recorded history for us. There are pictures from many sources, and I am so grateful to them all, for their work, foresight, and diligence over the years; especially also for sharing their work and not keeping their images locked away.

Of course, it is not always possible to obtain perfect images of every bus operated and those included in the book are used to present a complete record as possible when alternative images could not be found. For me, the words are the easy part of a book, finding right images is the hardest part; as my gravestone may well say, "He tried". Having said this, research never finishes as there are always "some gaps." Therefore, if anyone can assist to fill in such gaps, then I will be delighted to hear from you.

My royalties from the book sales, after deduction of costs, are going 100% to assist on bus preservation/archives. I, and some of the image providers, have supplied their services free of charge to help this initiative.

Text © Stuart Emmett, 2021.
First published in the United Kingdom, 2021,
by Stenlake Publishing Ltd.,
54-58 Mill Square,
Catrine, Ayrshire,
KA5 6RD

Telephone: 01290 551122
www.stenlake.co.uk

ISBN 9781840339147

The publishers regret that they cannot supply copies of any pictures featured in this book.

Picture Acknowledgements

Unless stated below, the pictures are from my own collection that is made up of our family pictures and other sources, some of which have proved impossible to identify. For these, I offer my apologies for the lack of accreditation and ask that the publisher be contacted in the first instance.

Pictures/images are from the following people, and in no specific order:

Peter Hirst: page 14.
Roy Marshall: pages 7, 18, 23 (both), 25, 31, 32, 33, 35, 36, 40, 44 (upper).
Roger Holmes: pages 19, 20 (both), 24, 29, 30 (lower).
RHG Simpson: page 28 (lower).
Tony Greaves: pages 37, 39/back cover, 41 (both), 42 (upper), 45/front cover, 46, 47, 48.
Robert Mack: page 15.
Peter Henson: page 38.

Also, from the following image providers:

Mineralcraft: page 14.
The Bus Archive: pages 19, 20 (both), 23 (both), 24, 25, 30 (lower), 31, 32, 33, 35, 36, 40, 44 (upper).
P.M. Photography: pages 26, 42 (lower).
Travel Lens Photographic: pages 28 (upper), 44 (lower).

References

Commercial Motor on the 8th February 1952.
Harry & Kay Jordan, *Adventures of a Bus Driver*, 1992.
Leeds & District Transport News that became the *Metro Transport News*.

Overview

Called 'Ponty' by its citizens, Pontefract has been a market town since the Middle Ages. It lies east of the Pennine foothills, and 4 miles south of the River Aire that runs just north of Castleford, with close proximity to the A1M and the M62.

Pontefract's deep, sandy soil was one of the few British places where liquorice could be successfully grown, and the town has a large liquorice confectionery industry where the famous Pontefract cakes are produced. Although the liquorice plant itself is no longer grown there and uses extract from Turkey, there are still two liquorice factories, one owned by Haribo (formerly Dunhill's) and one by Tangerine Confectionery (formerly part of Cadbury's and before that Wilkinson's). The Liquorice Festival is held annually in Pontefract. The town is also home to Pontefract Racecourse, the longest continuous flat racing circuit in Europe.

Up to the 1980s coal mining was an especially important industry in the whole area, from the north of Castleford to Selby in the east and to Wakefield in the west and down to Barnsley and Doncaster in the south. With numerous pits and close to the former large coal-fired power station at Ferrybridge on the A1M, most of the local coal mines were closed in the 1990s, contributing to high unemployment in the local area, with the final local colliery closing in August 2002.

The Wakefield, Leeds, and Doncaster boundary areas were served post-war by three independent bus companies, J. Bullock and Sons (1928) Limited of Featherstone, West Riding Automobile Company Limited of Wakefield, and South Yorkshire Motors Limited.

In the 1920s, J. Bullock & Sons Limited was facing strong competition from the West Riding Automobile Company. This caused friction within the Bullock family that culminated in expensive litigation and the separation of Ernest Bullock and his younger brother Jim.

Jim Bullock then formed J. Bullock and Sons (1928) Limited. Ernest Bullock left his brothers and in 1929 bought South Yorkshire which then became South Yorkshire Motors Limited (SYM).

J. Bullock & Sons (1928) Limited, trading as B&S Motor Services of Featherstone, carried on but were to sell out in 1950 to West Riding. Meanwhile Ernest Bullock gradually built up SYM with his son Reg and after Ernest's death in 1962 followed by his son in 1968, it was taken on by relatives. SYM became the South Yorkshire Road Transport (SYRT) in 1973. Whilst this part of the story is covered more fully in Part 2 of this book, in 1994, SYRT was sold to the Caldaire Group who also by now owned West Riding, as well as Selby & District and Yorkshire Woollen District from Dewsbury. The Caldaire Group then became the British Bus Group and, by 1998, were Cowie that was rebranded as Arriva.

With the above overview in mind, the development of the South Yorkshire bus company follows.

The Winder era 1925 to 1929 SYM Company

What became the South Yorkshire Motors Company, was started by Mrs May Winder in August 1925. Using a car and bus given by her husband, Raymond W. Winder, who worked in the legal profession, a bus service was started into Pontefract from Badsworth near to Thorpe Audlin, a small village 6 miles to the south of Pontefract. Another bus was purchased in the November and a third bus came on hire purchase in December 1925.

In April 1926 Badsworth Motor Company of The Garage, Thorpe Audlin was renamed as South Yorkshire Motor Company with partners from the Winder family; Mrs M, son Raymond and daughter Joan. Soon another bus came on hire purchase along with a service in 1926 to Doncaster via Barnsdale Bar and yet more buses also bought on hire purchase.

In September 1926 an ambitious Leeds to London via Pontefract service started (that was only licensed in September 1927).

Three American Studebaker "Big 6" models operated on the London services. WU7611 above was one of them and was new in July 1926, but had gone by December 1928, the others soon followed. Studebaker had a long history in the USA, starting with building horse-drawn vehicles, then electric cars in the early 1900s. They were the third largest US car manufacturer by 1913. Commercial vehicles followed in 1920s. The four with South Yorkshire would have been an enormous gamble for a small UK company.

A view of the SYM operation at this time is available from a former driver:

> "The company I was working for in 1927 was South Yorkshire Motor Co, and the owner was a Mrs Winder. At the time we thought nothing of it, but looking back, it seems a strange business for a woman to be involved in, especially as her husband was a King's Counsel and she probably had no need to work. Perhaps she was ahead of her time and believed women were as capable as men at running a business, but she certainly did not look like a typical feminist: she was a bit like the Queen Mum in appearance and she had a warm smile and a kind word for all her employees. What is more to the point she paid well and those of us who had to drive the real wrecks got five shillings a week extra.
>
> Having done that, however, she seemed to think her responsibility was at an end, for not a penny was spent on the upkeep of those buses except in cases of dire emergency.
>
> I think I could write a whole book on this topic, for a more broken-down dilapidated fleet of buses you would not see outside a wrecker's yard. There were three or four Studebakers from the year dot, an Italian model and a few other machines, same era. The few roadworthy models were reserved for the daily Leeds to London run and a monthly run to Brussels. Any of the drivers who had mechanical experience, as I had, were expected to drive the cast-offs".

(*Adventures of a Bus Driver*, 1992)

In August 1928, the Leeds agents for the London service started a service themselves, and SYM started to lose money. Undeterred it seems, SYM applied to increase the Leeds to Doncaster service to every 30 minutes and four buses were acquired. The application, after an inquiry, was granted. Meanwhile, in November 1928 the bus services reported as running were:

- Leeds – Pontefract – Barnsdale Bar – Doncaster hourly
- Pontefract – Askern – Doncaster every 90 mins
- Leeds – Pontefract – Doncaster – London once a day

1929 saw an attempt to form a limited company and by this time 15 vehicles were on hire purchase. SYM however had financial problems and their accountants wrote to creditors asking for a 12 months credit extension, the company having a reported £54.10 in assets and a deficit of £10,046. These problems were noticed by observers and on 26th June 1929 the business was sold to Mr. E. P. Bullock and his son J. R. Bullock.

They added four buses to the SY fleet along with the Bullock buy of the Weaver Bus Company that traded as the Blue Bus company who ran from Pontefract to Barnsley via Ackworth and who had gone into liquidation in summer 1929. It is thought that Bullock also bought Hallamshire Transport Co of Hemsworth, owned by Mrs Winder's husband, Edmund Alfred Winder, and that this company was absorbed in 1930.

The Bullock era 1929 to 1968 SYM Limited

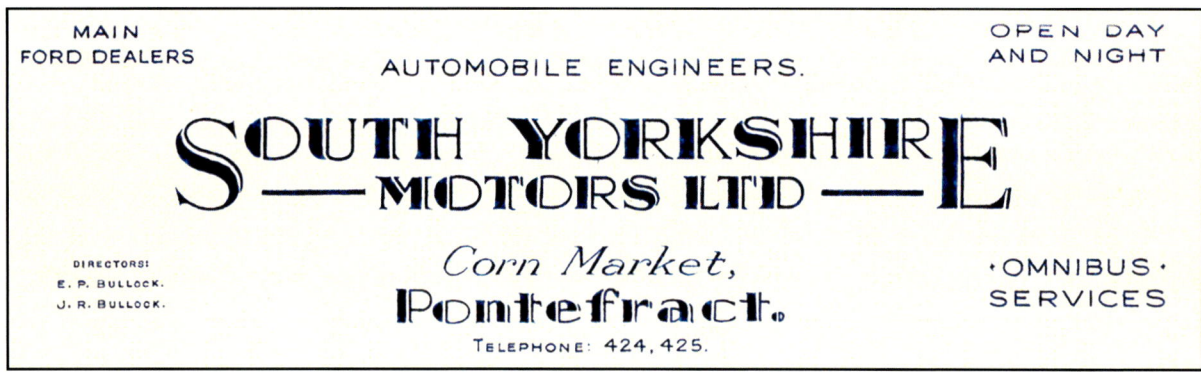

South Yorkshire Motors Limited was formed in July 1930 with an address at Cornmarket, Pontefract. This was the former Pontefract base of J. Bullock and Sons (B&S Motors) and now became the SY base. B&S Motors had been formed in 1913 by the Bullock Brothers, but friction had led Ernest Bullock and his son Reg to leave and buy SYM. Alternatively, it was also reported that Mr. E. P. Bullock had actually retired from B&S and was looking for a company to develop.

Other services were soon started; these were in 1929 to Whitley Bridge and Selby. Colliery services were also operated as was a summer express from Barnsley to Bridlington from 1934, which stopped in 1940 and then never restarted after the war.

As car travel was growing, then car sales and dealerships with Morris and Ford were started in Pontefract and later, in Wakefield and Castleford. This was destined to become a major part of the company and would also include Ford's range of tractors and agricultural equipment.

The earlier 1926 London service started by South Yorkshire was also expanded to start in Bradford by April 1928 and in 1929 they cooperated with B&E Ltd (Heath and Ennifer) of Doncaster. South Yorkshire also bought the Wilke Parlour Car Services in Leeds. This cooperative joint venture was named London. Midland and Yorkshire Services Limited and ran three services a day to London.

The development of the London routes is an interesting story. This short-lived coach route to London only ran between 1926 and 1934; the following is a summary:

- May 1927 London (Southampton Row) to Leeds via the A1 to Doncaster then via Pontefract into Leeds, running on two days a week, leaving London on Tuesday/Friday at 0900 and Leeds on Sunday/Wednesday at 0830. This was probably the first route between the two cities.
- October 1927 a departure from each terminus at 0900 hours.
- April 1928 a short-lived extension to Bradford leaving at 0830 hours for Leeds.

Reo Pullman WX1531 came in August 1929 with a Harrison of Dewsbury 20-seater body. Three more US made Reo came in August/September 1929 ordered before the Bullock takeover. Two stayed until September 1933, the third until August 1935, by which time new Albions were being considered. Roy Marshall Collection

- April 1930 a daily service started leaving Leeds at 0918 and London at 0900 with additional night buses on Wednesday/Friday/Saturday leaving at Leeds at 2318 hours and London at 2330 hours. The journey time was around 9/10 hours with the timetables noting the arrival on the morning departures at "about tea time".

- 1932 advertised daily routes with Leeds departures at 0900 arriving at 1815, and from London at 0945, arriving in Leeds at 1900 hours.

In the early 1930s modern and larger vehicles were being used by the Doncaster branch of the London service joint venture.

Arising from the 1929 formation of London, Midland and Yorkshire Services Limited, Doncaster became an interchange from where numerous extensions were advertised. There was now the existing one using the A1, and an additional one via the Midlands.

The illustration shows the extent of the operation in 1933 with Doncaster as the centre of operations, with an all-year day service, and night buses in summer and at Christmas.

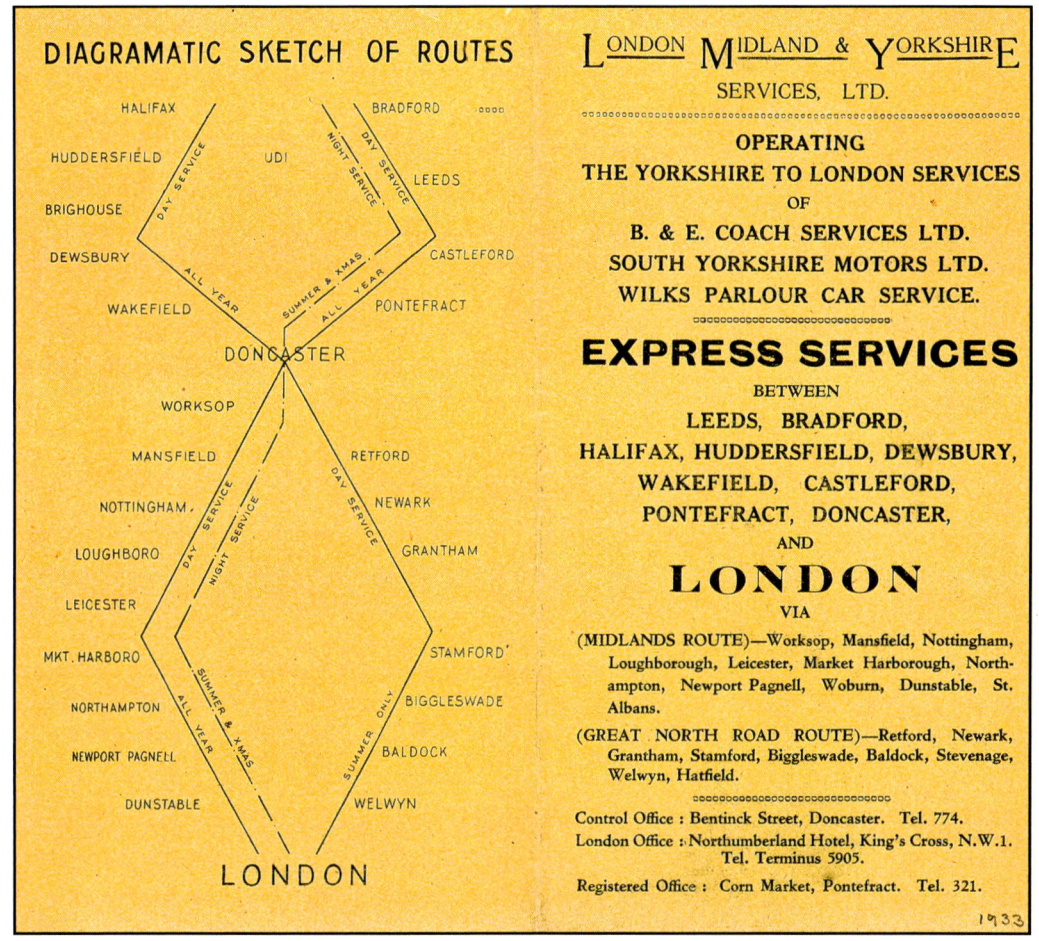

In November 1934 West Yorkshire Road Car bought the London, Midland and Yorkshire Services operation, on behalf of the newly-formed express service group, Yorkshire Services. A bold pioneering operation was therefore finished after just eight years. Meanwhile, the 1920s stage routes carried onto the 1930s, with Albions now being the vehicle of choice.

For the stage buses at Pontefract, Albions were favoured from 1929 to 1950 as shown in this 1932 advertisement.

The Second World War reduced frequencies on routes and early post-war route developments were few, with only the 1954 route to Ferrybridge via Chequerfield. From 1955, in recognition of operating long routes, double-deckers were fitted for comfort with dual-purpose type seats, electrically-operated doors, and decorative interior panelling.

Ernest Bullock died in 1962 and was followed by his son, Reg, the long serving Managing Director, who died in 1968. The company carried on as before under John McCloy, a grandson of Ernest Bullock, until major changes were made in 1973, which are covered in Part 2 of this book.

Stage Routes Development

For completeness, this includes the 1973 to 1975 developments.

From	To	Via	Start	Headway in 1968	Trip time	Comments
Pontefract	Badsworth	East Hardwick, Thorpe Audlin.	November 1925	n/a	n/a	Into Doncaster service (see below).
Pontefract	Doncaster	East Hardwick, Thorpe Audlin, Barnsdale Bar, Red House, Highfields.	October 1926. September 1927 was on the licence.	Hourly	42 minutes	WYPTE route 410. *
Pontefract	Leeds	Glass Houghton, Cutsyke, Whitwood, Methley, Stourton.	September 1927	Hourly	43 minutes	Linked to Doncaster Barnsdale Bar. * WYPTE route 410.
Pontefract	Doncaster	Ferrybridge, Knottingley, Cridling Stubbs, Askern, Bentley – "The country route".	December 1927	Hourly	75 minutes	** WYPTE route 411.
Pontefract	Barnsley	Purston, Ackworth, Brackenhill, Nostell Priory, Hemsworth, Shafton, Cudworth.	September 1929	Hourly to Barnsley and hourly shorts to Hemsworth. By 1968 a 2-minute extension from Hemsworth to the Highfield Estate.	65 minutes and 38 minutes.	Circa 1934 joint with YTC route 45. Later WYPTE 245.

Headway and journey times are mainly from the 1968 timetable.

* Linked operationally Pontefract to Doncaster via Barnsdale, Pontefract to Leeds and Pontefract (Cobblers Lane) to Leeds.

** Linked operationally Pontefract to Doncaster via Askern and Pontefract to Knottingley (Broomhill).

From	To	Via	Start	Headway in 1968	Trip time	Comments
Pontefract	Selby or Hut Green at Whitley Bridge.	Nevison, Ferrybridge, Knottingley, Beal, Killington, Hut Green, Burn, Brayton.	October 1929	Every 2 hours	51 minutes 29 minutes	To Selby – Saturday/Sunday/Monday only. To Hut Green – Tuesday to Friday only. WYPTE route 486.
Barnsley, Hemsworth and Pontefract.	Bridlington	Ferrybridge, Knottingley, Hut Green, Snaith, Goole – Summer only service.	May 1934	Wednesday/Saturday/Sunday. Three a day.	3 hours 45 minutes	Finished August 1940 and never restarted.
Pontefract	Pinders Garth, Ferrybridge.	Chequerfield	August 1954	Monday to Saturday, hourly.	13 minutes	WYPTE route 487.
Pontefract Cobbler Lane Estate	Leeds	Western Avenue, Northfield, Glass Houghton, Methley, Stourton, Hunslet.	June 1974	Hourly Monday to Saturday. Sunday and evening runs only from Pontefract to Cobblers Lane.	33 minutes	Limited Stop aka Timesaver from Glass Houghton to Leeds. *
Pontefract	Knottingley Broomhill Avenue	Nevison, Ferrybridge.	May 1975	Hourly and scheduled in with the Doncaster-Askern service.	18 minutes	WYPTE route 488. **

Headway and journey times are mainly from the 1968 timetable.

* Linked operationally Pontefract to Doncaster via Barnsdale, Pontefract to Leeds and Pontefract (Cobblers Lane) to Leeds.

** Linked operationally Pontefract to Doncaster via Askern and Pontefract to Knottingley (Broomhill).

From	To	Via	Start	Headway in 1968	Trip time	Comments
Pontefract	Manchester	Glass Houghton, Castleford, Whitwood, Normanton, M62, Prestwich.	September 1975	Initially two journeys daily, then from October 1978, just one journey Monday/Thursday/Friday.	90 minutes	Finished January 1980.
Castleford	Hull	Glass Houghton, Pontefract, Ferrybridge Knottingley, Whitley Bridge, M62, Hessle.	September 1975	Initially two journeys daily, then from October 1978, one journey on Tuesday/Wednesday/Saturday.	90 minutes	Finished January 1980.

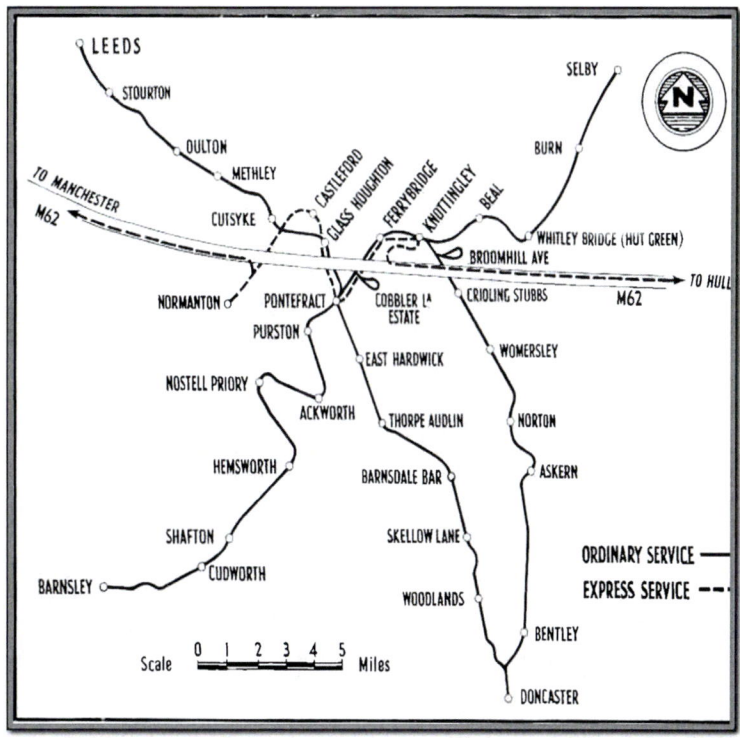

Fleet in service from 1950

The Stage fleet was renewed around every two years, and SY usually bought 2/3 buses at the same time. However, the coaches bought from 1973 onwards came as they were needed.

35 WX2326 in Doncaster was an Albion new in November 1929 but with a Burlingham B32F body from early 1943. Seen in Doncaster it was withdrawn in 1950 and used as a service vehicle until December 1956. Peter Hirst/Mineralcraft

43 AWR580 was 1935 Albion Valkyrie with an English Electric body. Withdrawn in January 1954, it went to Wakefield Shirt Company t/a Double Two, the destination for many of SY buses. RF Mack

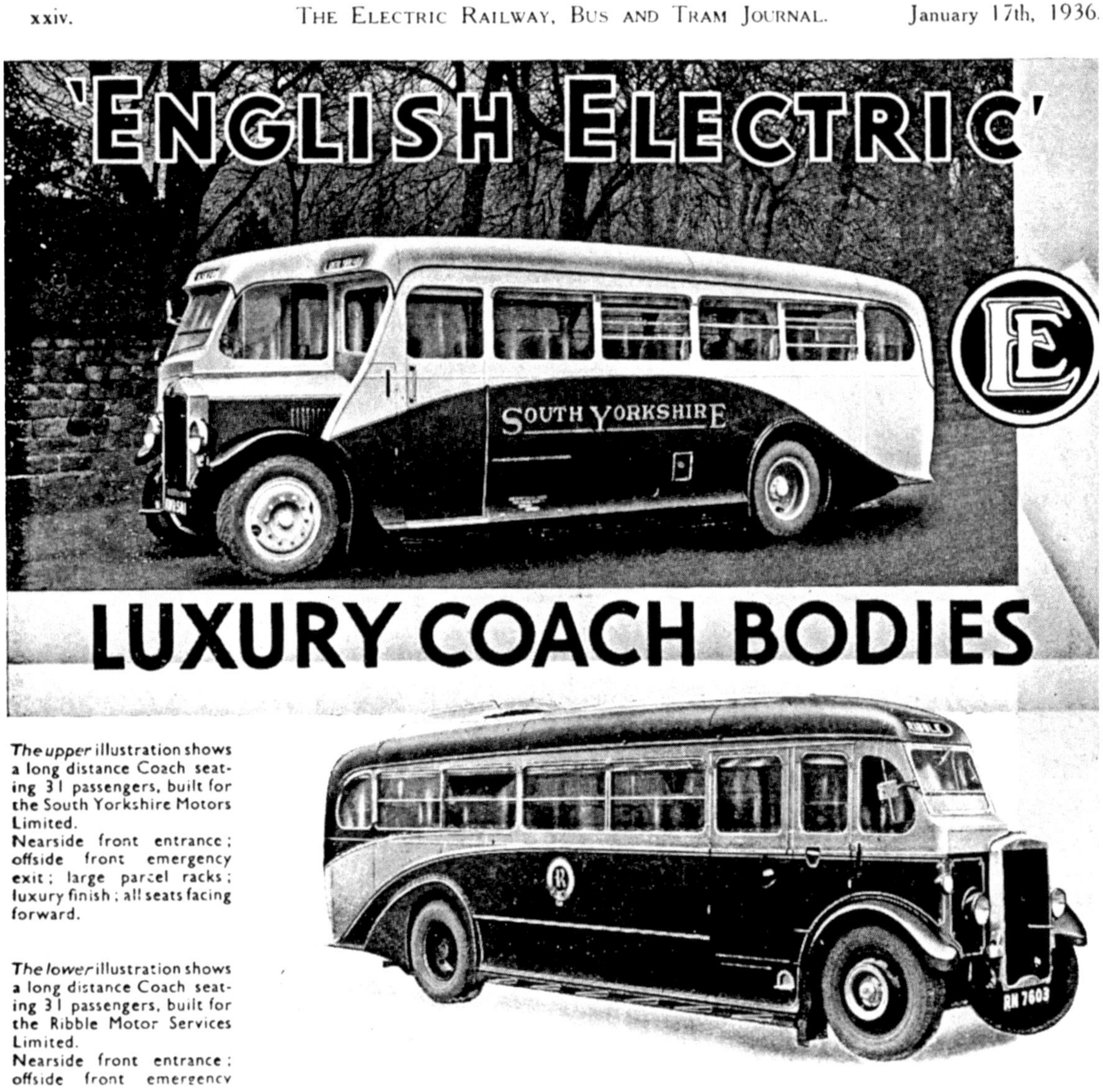
xxiv. THE ELECTRIC RAILWAY, BUS AND TRAM JOURNAL. January 17th, 1936.

The upper illustration shows a long distance Coach seating 31 passengers, built for the South Yorkshire Motors Limited.
Nearside front entrance; offside front emergency exit; large parcel racks; luxury finish; all seats facing forward.

The lower illustration shows a long distance Coach seating 31 passengers, built for the Ribble Motor Services Limited.
Nearside front entrance; offside front emergency

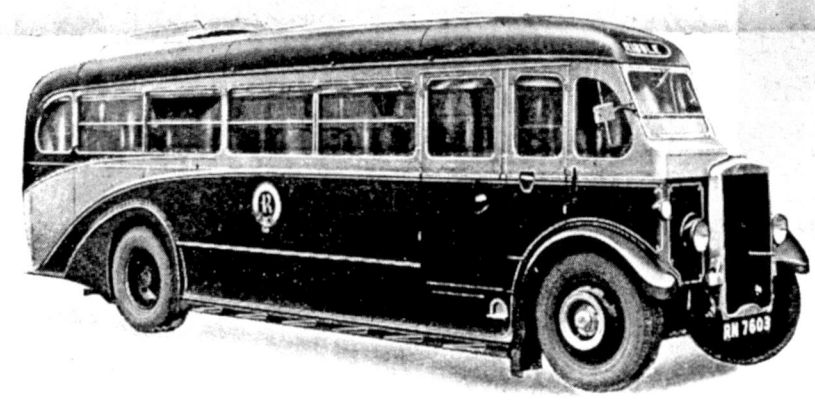

44 AWR581 was an Albion Valkyrie with English Electric body new in 1936 and featured in English Electric advertising. It was withdrawn in October 1951 and went to a contractor in Knottingley.

46 AWY948 as AWY576 (a fake number plate for the Olympia exhibition/show) 46 was an Albion Valkyrie with English Electric body new in 1936 and thought to have been withdrawn in October 1951 when it went to Wakefield Shirt Company.

47 BWY438 was another Albion Valkyrie with English Electric body new in 1937 and seen here at Pontefract depot with 49, (seen in the next picture) and the rear of 35 (shown earlier). 47 was withdrawn in October 1957 and sold onto Wakefield Shirt. R. Marshall

Albion Valkyrie 49 CWW374 with Burlingham C35F body from 1938. Withdrawn in December 1957 and sold to Wakefield Shirt. Roger Holmes/The Bus Archive

51 was another Albion Valkyrie with Duple B35F body to the Red & White style from 1941. In September 1956 the body was removed when it then gained the body from 57 and was also renumbered 57. The chassis of the original 57 then became double-decker 81. Roger Holmes/The Bus Archive

Duple bodied 54 came in April 1944 and was an early withdrawal in March 1955. The four-utility double-deckers (52 to 55) were progressively rebuilt. It is possible that not all four had all of the three rebuilds mentioned below. Duple 52 (left) is seen after the first one. Roger Holmes/The Bus Archive

The first rebuild covered:
- Radiused first and last saloon windows to give strength.
- Top slider windows fitted

The next rebuild and seen on 52 below, involved:
- Rubberised front lower saloon window
- Rubberised destination screens
- Rubberised front upper windows
- Rear illuminated number plate boxes
- High backed seats

The final changes are on 53 below:
- Livery to match the 1951 Leylands 73 to 76
- SY illuminated glass, introduced in 1955 by 77/78

Duple bodied 52 had been the first double-decker in October 1943 and is seen after the second rebuilding, with the rear of Brush 55 showing the rear registration number box rebuild. 52 was withdrawn in December 1960 and went to Wakefield Shirt. Also partly shown is the rear of Albion single-decker 59. The Bus Archive/Roy Marshall

Daimler CWA6/Brush numbered 53 & 55 (EWT956 & EWU772). Brush 53 seen above was delivered in March 1944 and stayed the longest of the Daimlers until February 1963 and is possibly seen just after delivery. However, another poor-quality photograph of an unknown utility taken in 1946, shows a different livery of a light colour (blue?) extended from the roof down to the upper deck window frames, then a white looking band, then a dark colour (blue) with another white band above the lower windows (as on 53 above), then with a light colour (blue?) lower window frames, and finally, the band and dark colour (as on 53 above).

Doncaster with Brush 53 after its first rebuild but still with the original destination screen. The Bus Archive/Roy Marshall

Brush 55 EWU772 and is seen after its first rebuild in Doncaster. The Bus Archive/Roy Marshall

Brush 55 in 1957 at Doncaster after its second rebuilding. Roger Holmes/The Bus Archive

Brush 55 is seen in Pontefract after its second rebuilding. It was withdrawn in June 1960 and likely did not receive the SY front glass or the 1951 livery. R. Marshall

Brush 53 EWT956 came in March 1944 and was the longest in service, being withdrawn in February 1963. 53 is alongside a Yorkshire Traction Leyland/Roe in Pontefract and seen here after the final rebuild. PM Photography

56, GWT631 was new in December 1957 and was Albion/5 bay Strachan. It was withdrawn in February 1963.

56, GWT631 is seen after being rebuilt when it had received:

- A whole body rebuild.
- Drip rails removed.
- Rubberised windows and screens
- Livery to match the 1951 Leylands 73 to 76.
- SY illuminated glass, introduced in 1955 by 77/78

Travel Lens Photographic

57 was delivered in January 1950 and was an Albion Valkyrie with Burlingham coach body. In 1957 the body went to 51 and this bus was renumbered as 57. Meanwhile the chassis of 57 was refurbished and became 81 TWY8 and as seen later, gained a Roe double-deck body. RHG Simpson

The "new" 57 with the chassis from 51, was withdrawn in March 1964 and went for preservation. Roger Holmes/The Bus Archive

58 to 60 were Albion Valkyries new in December 1945 (with 60 new in January 1946) and had Pickering B34F bodies, Withdrawn respectively in February 1960, January 1958, and October 1957, both 58 and 60 went to Wakefield Shirt. 60 (left) is seen outside the offices in Pontefract.

The batch was progressively rebuilt as follows:

- side windows with top sliders
- drip strips removed.
- illuminated duplicate sign at n/s fitted.
- destination screen rubber glazed.
- possibly retro fitted with porch style entrance, maybe had from new?

59 in Pontefract before some of the rebuilding.
Roger Holmes/The Bus Archive

Parked in Leeds Bus Station when likely working as a duplicate, Albion Valkyrie/Burlingham C33F fleet number 61 was new in December 1947 and worked until August 1967 when it went into preservation. The Bus Archive/Roy Marshall

61 being washed with the "original" 51 in the right background with Leyland 75 and Albion 70. Three Ford cars can be seen, two of which look unregistered, clearly connected to the "main business" of the Ford dealership. The Bus Archive/Roy Marshall

The last Albions came in February 1950 and were 70 to 72 JWR873 to 875. Albion Venturers with 4 bay Strachan bodies, they were originally like 70 above seen in Doncaster. The Bus Archive/Roy Marshall

The 70 to 72 batch was rebuilt and 70, again in Doncaster is seen on the left.

The rebuilding covered the following:

- Whole body rebuild.
- Drip rails removed.
- Rubberised windows and screens
- Driver's door
- Livery to match the 1951 Leylands 73 to 76.
- SY illuminated glass, introduced in 1955 by 77/78

70 was withdrawn in April 1965 and was another one for Wakefield Shirt with 71/72 going in June 1967.

Nearside view of 71 nicely showing the starting handle in a leather strap. Roy Marshall/The Bus Archive

73 to 76 were delivered in October 1951 (KWU978/9) and November 1951 (KWY223/4). They were Leyland PD2/12 with Leyland bodywork and were delivered in a plain primer. The batch introduced this specific livery style and also were the last buses with open rear platforms. They later had the SY front glasses fitted. 75 is seen in Doncaster. The Bus Archive/Roy Marshall

74 enters entering Pontefract Bus Station now with SY front glasses. It was withdrawn in July 1973 after an accident. Tony Greaves

The fatal accident damage to 74. Peter Henson/The Bus Archive

75 leans into Leeds Bus Station and worked until October 1974. 75/76 had a band below the lower windows that 73/74 did not have. Tony Greaves

77/78 registered OWR264/5 were Leyland PD2/20 with rare Bond bodies and were delivered in August and September 1955. With dual-purpose seats, decorative interior panelling and with rear platform doors (the first in the fleet), they worked until August and September 1975 and were then replaced by secondhand AEC single-deckers from YWD/Hebble numbered 8/9 (KCP808/9G). 78 above is at Leeds with its original upper windows. 77/78 were the first buses delivered with upper SY window glass, these then being retro fitted to the earlier Albion and Leyland double-deckers. Roy Marshal/The Bus Archive

77 now with the upper front window ventilators removed. Tony Greaves

79/80 (TWY6/7) Leyland PD2/20 with Park Royal L53RD bodies were new in November 1957. 79 loads at Pontefract Bus Station for Broomhill. Tony Greaves

79, with its high-backed seats, was withdrawn in August 1983.
Tony Greaves

81 was a hybrid that entered service in May 1958 and was an Albion CX39N with Roe L53RD body. The chassis was originally new in 1950 as single-decker 57 (JWT112) with a Burlingham coach body. This chassis was rebuilt to become 81 and the single-deck coach body from 57 went to the chassis of 51 that was now renumbered 57.

Large local companies like Yorkshire Traction, Yorkshire Woollen, Wallace Arnold, and West Riding had many double-decker rebuilds from single-deckers; CIE, UTA, PMT, Alexander and Barton were others.

PM Photography

81 (when preserved) after being withdrawn in April 1971.

82 heads for Doncaster with a fated West Riding Guy Wulfrunian behind; these gave a smooth pleasing ride when they were new and when they ran "on form". As we will see in Part 2, this increasingly became not often! Roy Marshall / The Bus Archive.

84/85 390/1 CWT were Leyland Atlanteans with MCW L73F bodies new in January 1963 This body normally had 78 seats. They replaced 1943 Daimler 53 (the last of the wartime Daimlers) and 1947 Albion 56.

84 (left) is as delivered. Both 84/85 later had changed windscreen and the front opening upper windows removed.

Travel Lens Photographic

Two more Atlantean/MCWs came in January 1965 and were 86/87 (EWR486/7C). 86 has arrived in Leeds and is as delivered before slight body changes.
Tony Greaves

87 now with no front upper opening windows and flat windscreens. Tony Greaves

88/89 (PWR988/9E) were more Atlanteans, this time with Roe H70F bodies and came in May 1967. 88/89 left early in July and December 1978 due to bodywork problems. SY's body allegiances then passed to Northern Counties. 88 is seen as delivered. Tony Greaves

90/91 (HWR690/1J) and again, Atlanteans, but the first with Northern Counties bodies. Registered on 1st February 1971, 91 is at Leeds Bus Station and was the last bus delivered in this livery; it got the new livery, shown in Part2, in January 1975. SY reported being happy with Northern Counties over their standard of build, as well as having a friendly nature that was "like dealing with a family firm". Tony Greaves

The next batch of buses came in 1973 and are covered in the Part 2 book that covers the period from 1973 to 1994: "The Final Years and Reflections".